HOMEGIRLS
&
HANDGRENADES

HOMEGIRLS
&
HANDGRENADES

Sonia Sanchez

Beacon Press
Boston

BEACON PRESS
Boston, Massachusetts
www.beacon.org

Beacon Press books
are published under the auspices of
the Unitarian Universalist Association of Congregations.

26 25 24 23   8 7 6 5 4 3 2 1

This book is printed on acid-free paper that meets the uncoated paper
ANSI/NISO specifications for permanence as revised in 1992.

Text design and composition by Kim Arney

Library of Congress Cataloging-in-Publication Data

Names: Sanchez, Sonia, 1934– author.
Title: Homegirls & handgrenades / Sonia Sanchez.
Description: Boston : Beacon Press, [2023] | Series: Celebrating
Blackwomen writers | Summary: "Winner of the
American Book Award. A classic
of the Black Arts Movement brought back to life in
a refreshed edition"— Provided by publisher.
Identifiers: LCCN 2022053701 (print) | LCCN 2022053702 (ebook) |
ISBN 9780807012956 (trade paperback ; acid-free paper) |
ISBN 9780807012963 (ebook)
Subjects: LCGFT: Poetry.
Classification: LCC PS3569.A468 H64 2023 (print) |
LCC PS3569.A468 (ebook) | DDC 811/.54—dc23/eng/20221114
LC record available at https://lccn.loc.gov/2022053701
LC ebook record available at https://lccn.loc.gov/2022053702

To Anita, Morani and Mungu.
Much love!

CONTENTS

HOMEGIRLS
&
HANDGRENADES

THE POWER OF LOVE

un corazón solitario
no es un corazón

—ANTONIO MACHADO

POEM NO. 10

you keep saying you were always there
waiting for me to see you.
                        you said that once
on the wings of a pale green butterfly
you rode across san francisco's hills
and touched my hair as i caressed
a child called militancy
you keep saying you were always there

holding my small hand
                        as i walked
unbending indiana streets i could not see around
and you grew a black mountain
of curves and i turned
and became soft again
you keep saying you were always there

repeating my name softly
                        as i slept in
slow pittsburgh blues and you made me
sweat nite dreams that danced
and danced until the morning
rained yo/red delirium

you keep saying you were always there
you keep saying you were always there
will you stay love
now that i am here

WELCOME HOME,
MY PRINCE

welcome home, my prince
into my white season of no you
       welcome home
to my songs
that touch yo/head
       and rain green laughter
       in greeting
welcome home
to this monday
       that has grown up
with the sound of yo/name,
for i have chanted to yesterday's sun
to hurry back with
his belly full of morning
       and you have come
and i cannot look up at you.
       my body
trembles and i mumble things as you
stand tall and sacred
so easily in yo/self
       but i am here

to love you
          to carry yo/name on my
ankles like bells
          to dance in
yo/arena of love.
you are tattooed on the round/soft/
parts of me.
          and yo/smell is
always with me.

AFTER THE FIFTH DAY

with you
i pressed the
rose you bought me
into one of fanon's books
it has no odor now.
                    but
i see you handing me a red
rose and i remember
my birth.

HAIKU

your love was a port
of call where many ships docked
until morning came

STORY

in medias res
there came a man into the city
he wore a jackdaw face
and loved the glittering town.
i cannot say why he chose me.
i was the city's device
the city's kept disgrace.
yet he lifted me until i had
a passion to please
all displeasures.

each day he said
o my child,
the world has moved away from love
the earth has moved away from worship
i am destined to end their exile.

         and he returned me to the mainland
         dressed in white. i was in unity.
         soon, o soon, i would be worthy.
because he was good with his hands
he became a technician
where mathematical abstractions
were operable.

thus he caressed two levers that could level

three generations of russians

resting in their squares.

each day he cried

when will they understand the

errors of their ways

when will they touch the godhead

and leave the verses of the rocks?

> and i was dressed in blue
>
> blue of the savior's sky
>
> soon, o soon, i would be worthy.

there are many cities

there are men in the cities

rooted.

there are few men

there are few cities

afraid.

there are cities

crowded with christs

invisible

there are men

crystal with echoes

indifferent

there are many cities

there are men in the cities

empty

there are few cities
there are few men
worthy.

soon, o soon, I would be worthy.

ringaroundtheatmosphere
apocketfullofchains
kerboomkerboom
wehavenopains

HAIKU

we are sudden stars
you and i exploding
in our blue black skins

"JUST DON'T NEVER GIVE UP ON LOVE"

Feeling tired that day, I came to the park with the children. I saw her as I rounded the corner, sitting old as stale beer on the bench, ruminating on some uneventful past. And I thought, "Hell. No rap from the roots today. I need the present. On this day. This Monday. This July day buckling me under her summer wings, I need more than old words for my body to squeeze into."

I sat down at the far end of the bench, draping my legs over the edge, baring my back to time and time unwell spent. I screamed to the children to watch those curves threatening their youth as they rode their 10-speed bikes against mid-western rhythms.

I opened my book and began to write. They were coming again, those words insistent as his hands had been, pounding inside me, demanding their time and place. I relaxed as my hands moved across the paper like one possessed.

I wasn't sure just what it was I heard. At first I thought it was one of the boys calling me so I kept on writing. They knew the routine by now. Emergencies demanded a presence. A facial confrontation. No long distance screams across trees and space and other children's screams. But the sound pierced the pages and I looked around, and there she was inching her bamboo-creased body toward my back, coughing a beaded sentence off her tongue.

"Guess you think I ain't never loved, huh girl? Hee. Hee. Guess that what you be thinking, huh?"

I turned. Startled by her closeness and impropriety, I stuttered, "I, I, I, Whhhaat dooooo you mean?"

"Hee. Hee. Guess you think I been old like this fo'ever, huh?" She leaned toward me, "Huh? I was so pretty that mens brought me breakfast in bed. Wouldn't let me hardly do no work at all."

"That's nice ma'am. I'm glad to hear that." I returned to my book. I didn't want to hear about some ancient love that she carried inside her. I had to finish a review for the journal. I was already late. I hoped she would get the hint and just sit still. I looked at her out of the corner of my eye.

"He could barely keep hisself in changing clothes. But he was pretty. My first husband looked like the sun. I used to say his name over and over again 'til it hung from my ears like diamonds. Has you ever loved a pretty man, girl?"

I raised my eyes, determined to keep a distance from this woman disturbing my day.

"No ma'am. But I've seen many a pretty man. I don't like them though cuz they keep their love up high in a linen closet and I'm too short to reach it."

Her skin shook with laughter.

"Girl you gots some spunk about you after all. C'mon over here next to me. I wants to see yo' eyes up close. You looks so uneven sittin' over there."

Did she say uneven? Did this old buddah splintering death say uneven? Couldn't she see that I had one eye shorter than the other; that my breath was painted on porcelain; that one breast crocheted keloids under this white blouse?

I moved toward her though. I scooped up the years that had stripped me to the waist and moved toward her. And she called to me to come out, come out wherever you are young woman, playing hide and go seek with scarecrow men. I gathered myself up at the gateway of her confessionals.

"Do you know what it mean to love a pretty man, girl?" She crooned in my ear. "You always running behind a man like that girl while he cradles his privates. Ain't no joy in a pretty yellow man, cuz he always out pleasurin' and givin' pleasure."

I nodded my head as her words sailed in my ears. Here was the pulse of a woman whose black ass shook the world once.

She continued. "A woman crying all the time is pitiful. Pitiful I says. I wuz pitiful sitting by the window every night like a cow in the fields chewin' on cud. I wanted to cry out, but not even God hisself could hear me. I tried to cry out til my mouth wuz split open at the throat. I 'spoze there is a time all womens has to visit the slaughter house. My visit lasted five years."

Touching her hands, I felt the summer splintering in prayer; touching her hands, I felt my bones migrating in red noise. I asked, "When did you see the butterflies again?"

Her eyes wandered like quicksand over my face. Then she smiled, "Girl don't you know yet that you don't never give up on love? Don't you know you has in you the pulse of winds? The noise of dragonflies?" Her eyes squinted close and she said, "One of them mornings he woke up callin' me and I wuz gone. I wuz gone running with the moon over my shoulders. I looked no which way at all. I had inside me 'nough knives and spoons to cut/scoop out the night. I wuz a tremblin' as I met the mornin'."

She stirred in her 84-year-old memory. She stirred up her body as she talked. "They's men and mens. Some good. Some bad. Some breathing death. Some breathing life. William woz my beginnin'. I come to my second husband spittin' metal and he just pick me up and fold me inside him. I wuz christen' with his love."

She began to hum. I didn't recognize the song; it was a prayer. I leaned back and listened to her voice rustling like silk. I heard cathedrals and sonnets; I heard tents and revivals and a black woman spilling black juice among her ruins.

"We all gotta salute death one time or 'nother girl. Death be waitin' outdoors trying to get inside. William died at his job. Death just turned 'round and snatched him right off the street."

Her humming became the only sound in the park. Her voice moved across the bench like a mutilated child. And I cried. For myself. For this woman talkin' about love. For all the women who have ever stretched their bodies out anticipating civilization and finding ruins.

The crashing of the bikes was anticlimactic. I jumped up, rushed toward the accident. Man. Little man. Where you bicycling to so very fast? Man. Second little man. Take it slow. It all passes so fast anyhow.

As I walked the boys and their bikes toward the bench, I smiled at this old woman waiting for our return.

"I want you to meet a great lady, boys."

"Is she a writer, too, ma?"

"No honey. She's a lady who has lived life instead of writing about it."

"After we say hello can we ride a little while longer? Please!"

"Ok. But watch your manners now and your bones afterwards."

"These are my sons, ma'am."

"How you do sons? I'm Mrs. Rosalie Johnson. Glad to meet you."

The boys shook her hand and listened for a minute to her words. Then they rode off, spinning their wheels on a city neutral with pain.

As I stood watching them race the morning, Mrs. Johnson got up.

"Don't go," I cried. "You didn't finish your story."

"We'll talk by-and-by. I comes out here almost everyday. I sits here on the same bench everyday. I'll probably die sittin' here one day. As good a place as any I 'magine."

"May I hug you, ma'am? You've helped me so much today. You've given me strength to keep on looking."

"No. Don't never go looking for love girl. Just wait. It'll come. Like the rain fallin' from the heaven, it'll come. Just don't never give up on love."

We hugged; then she walked her 84-year-old walk down the street. A black woman. Echoing gold. Carrying couplets from the sky to crease the ground.

BLUES
IS
BULLETS

cuidado: muerde

POEM WRITTEN AFTER READING WRIGHT'S "AMERICAN HUNGER"

for the homegirl who told Wright of her desire to go to the circus

such a simple desire
wanting to go to the circus
wanting to see the animals
orange with laughter.

such a simple need
amid yo /easy desire
to ride her
while clowns waited offstage
and children tugged at her young legs.

did you tell her man that we're
all acrobats tumbling out of
our separate arenas?
you. peeling her
skin while dreams turned
somersaults in her eyes.

such a simple woman
illiterate with juices
in a city where hunger
is passed around for seconds.

BLUES

i love a twenty yr old weekends
dig him way down until he's glad.
yeh. i love a twenty yr old weekends
dig him way down until he's glad
you see what my wanting you has
done gone and made me badddddd.

watched for you each evening
stood right outside my do
said i watched for you each evening
stood right outside my do
but you never came in and
i couldn't stand still no mo

what do you do when you need
a man so much it hurt?
i say where do you go when you
need a man so much it hurt?
you make it down to the corner
and start digging in the dirt.

yeh. i love a twenty yr old weekends
dig him way down until he's dry

yeh. i love a twenty yr old weekends
dig him way down until he's dry
you see what my needing you
has done gone and made me try.

you see what my needing you
has done gone and made me try.

NORMA

As a teenager I was very shy. I always felt so conspicuous that I talked with my head down, walked with my head down and would have slept with my head down if sleeping had demanded a standing position. It was with difficulty that I mustered up courage to ask Mr. Castor again and again, "But how do you factor that equation? I don't understand how it's done."

And he kept pointing to the book and looking upward, as if the combination of those actions would give me the immediate joy of an answer.

A sound from the back of the class made me turn around. It was the "people"—the "people" who sat in the back and talked when they wanted to, ate their lunches when they wanted to, and paid attention when they wanted to. They were paying attention to Mr. Castor and me. And I shook. I always wanted to be inconspicuous around the "people."

Odessa screamed, "Sit down Mr. Castor. You don't know crap. Norma, go up front and teach that little 'pip-squeak' how to do this Algebra."

As Mr. Castor moved to the sidelines, like some dejected player, Norma got up and began her slow walk up to the blackboard.

Have you ever seen a river curve back on itself? That was Norma as she walked on the edge of the classroom. She was heavy with white petticoats as she questioned, "Whatcha wanna know Sonia?"

Indeed. What did I want to know? It was all so very simple. I just wanted to know how to factor the problems so I could do my homework. Nothing else. I had a father waiting for me at home who would take no excuses concerning homework. He said, "The teachers are there. If you don't know, ask them. They know the answers." He didn't know Mr. Castor though.

As I asked the question, she sighed, and explained the factoring process in such an easy manner. I wrote it all down and closed my math notebook. I could do my homework now. There would be no problem with the family.

Norma was still at the blackboard. She hadn't moved and I knew that she was waiting for Lewis to say something. Lewis was the other brain in the class. They were always discussing some complex math problem. As if on cue, Lewis called out a more difficult question. She smiled. The smile ripened on her mouth like pomegranates.

Her fingers danced across the board. I watched her face. I was transfixed by her face that torpedoed the room with brilliance. She pirouetted problem after problem on the blackboard. We all thought genius. Norma is a mathematical genius.

I used to smile at Norma and sometimes she smiled back. She was the only one in the group who spoke to the "pip-squeaks" sitting up front. The others spoke, but it was usually a command of sorts. Norma would sometimes shake off her friends and sit down with the "pip-squeaks" and talk about the South. She was from Mississippi. She ordained us all with her red clay Mississippi talk. Her voice thawed us out from the merciless cold studding the hallways. Most of the time though, she laughed only with her teeth.

One day Norma called out a question in our French class. I understood part of the question. French was my favorite class. Mrs. LeFevebre was startled. She was a hunchback who swallowed her words so it was always difficult to understand her. But Norma's words were clear.

Mrs. LeFevebre spoke her well-digested English, "No rudeness, please Norma. You are being disrespectful. I shall not tolerate this."

Norma continued the conversation in French. Her accent was beautiful. I listened while her words fell like mangoes from her lips. The "people" laughed, "Talk that talk Norma. Go on girl. Keep on doin' it; whatever you're saying."

Mayhem. The smell of mayhem stalked the room. I wondered if the "people" would lock us all in the closet again.

Mrs. LeFevebre screamed, "Silence. Silence. Savages. How dare you ask me about my affliction. It is none of your business." As she talked, her large owl-head bobbed up and down on her waist. I wondered if she had trouble each night taking off her black dress. Her head was so large.

Norma stood up and started to pack her books. The noise subsided. She walked to the door, turned and said, "I just wanted to talk to you in your own language so you wouldn't be so lonely. You always look so lonely up there behind your desk. But screw you, you old bitch. You can go straight to hell for all I care. Hunchback and all."

She exited; the others followed, dragging their feet and mumbling black mourning words.

Mrs. LeFevebre stood still like a lizard gathering the sun.

I never liked that class after that. I still got good grades, but Norma, when she came to the French class, just sat and watched us struggle with our accents in amusement. I wondered what she did after school. I wondered if she ever studied.

George Washington High School was difficult. Our teachers had not prepared us for high school. The first year was catch-up time. My sister and I spent long nights in our small room, reading and studying our material.

I don't remember who it was. It was announced one day at lunchtime that Norma was pregnant. She had been dismissed from school. I had almost forgotten Norma. The mathematical genius. Norma. The linguist. The year had demanded so much work and old memories and faces had faded into the background.

I was rushing to the library. The library had become my refuge during the summer of '55. As I turned the corner of 145th Street, I heard her hello. Her voice was like stale music in barrooms. There she stood. Norma. Eyelids heavy. Woman of four children, with tracks running on her legs and arms.

"How you be doing Norma? You're looking good, girl."

"I'm making it Sonia. You really do look good, girl. Heard you went to Hunter College. Glad you made it."

"You should have gone too, Norma. You were the genius. The linguist. You were the brain. We just studied and got good grades. You were the one who understood it all."

And I started to cry. On that summer afternoon, I heard a voice from very far away paddling me home to a country of incense. To a country of red clay. I heard her laughter dancing with fireflies.

Tongue-tied by time and drugs, she smiled a funny smile and introduced me to her girls. Four beautiful girls. Norma predicted that they would make it. They wouldn't be like their mother. They would begin with a single step, then they would jump mountains.

I agreed.

She agreed.

We agreed to meet again.

Then I pulled myself up and turned away; never to agree again.

DEPRESSION

1.

i have gone into my eyes
bumping against sockets that sing
smelling the evening from under the sun
where waterless bones move
toward their rivers in incense.
a piece of light crawls up and down
then turns a corner.

as when drunken air molts in beds,
tumbling over blankets that cover sweat
nudging into sheets continuing dreams;
so i have settled in wheelbarrows
grotesque with wounds,
small and insistent as sleigh bells.

am i a voice delighting in the sand?
look how the masks rock on the winds
moving in tune to leaves.
i shed my clothes.
am i a seed consumed by breasts
without the weasel's eye
or the spaniel teeth of a child?

2.

i have cried all night
tears pouring out of my forehead
sluggish in pulse,
tears from a spinal soul
that run in silence to my birth
ayyyy! am i born? i cannot peel the flesh.
i hear the moon daring
to dance these rooms.
O to become a star.
stars seek their own mercy
and sigh the quiet, like gods.

BALLAD

(after the spanish)

forgive me if i laugh
you are so sure of love
you are so young
and i too old to learn of love.

the rain exploding
in the air is love
the grass excreting her
green wax is love
and stones remembering
past steps is love,
but you. you are too young
for love
and i too old.

once. what does it matter
when or who, i knew
of love.
i fixed my body
under his and went
to sleep in love
all trace of me
was wiped away

forgive me if i smile
young heiress of a naked dream
you are so young
and i too old to learn of love.

TO ALL BROTHERS:
FROM ALL SISTERS

each nite without you.

and i give birth to myself.

who am i to be touched at random?

to be alone so long. to see you move
in this varicose country
like silhouettes passing in apprenticeship,
from slave to slavery to pimp
to hustler to murderer to negro
to nigguhdom to militant to revolutionary
to blackness to faggot with the same
shadings of disrespect covering your voice.

and the nite, playing a maiden tune,
singes my eyes.

who am i to have loved you in rooms
lit by a single wall?
who am i to have loved at all as the
years come like water and the
madness of my blood drains rivers.

POEM NO. 12

when i am woman, then i shall be wife of your eyes
when i am woman, then i shall receive the sun
when i am woman, then i shall be shy with pain
when i am woman, then shall my laughter stop the wind
when i am woman, then i shall swallow the earth
when i am woman, then i shall give birth to myself
when i am woman, ay-y-y,ay-y-y,ay-y-y,
when i am woman. . .

A SONG

take my virginity
and convert it to maternity
wait around a century or two
and see just what I'll do.

take my body give it yo' brand
stitch my breasts on the fatherland
wait around a decade or two
and see just what i'll do.

place my dreams on any back stair
tune my eyes for yo' nightmare
wait around a century or two
and see what I'll finally do.

suck my breath until i stutter
listen to the sounds i utter
wait around a decade or two
and see just what i'll do.

take my daughter one sunday morn
drape her in dresses to be torn

wait around a century or two
and see what i'll finally do.

all dressed in white
find yourself a brand new wife
wait around a decade or two
and see what she'll finally do.
and see what she'll finally do.

AFTER SATURDAY NIGHT
COMES SUNDAY

I t had all started at the bank. She wuzn't sure, but she thot it had. At that crowded bank where she had gone to clear up the mistaken notion that she wuz $300.00 overdrawn in her checking account.

Sandy had moved into that undersized/low expectation of niggahs/being able to save anything bank/meanly. She wuz tired of people charging her fo they own mistakes. She had seen it wid her own eyes, five checks: four fo $50 the other one fo $100 made out to an Anthony Smith. It wuz Winston's signature. Her stomach jumped as she added and re-added the figures. Finally she dropped the pen and looked up at the business/suited/man sitten across from her wid crossed legs and eyes. And as she called him faggot in her mind, watermelon tears gathered round her big eyes and she just sat.

Someone had come for her at the bank. A friend of Winston's helped her to his car. It wuz the wite/dude who followed Winston constantly wid his eyes. Begging eyes she had once called em, half in jest, half seriously. They wuz begging now, along wid his mouth, begging Sandy to talk. But she cudn't. The words had gone away, gotten lost, drowned by the warm/april/rain dropping in on her as she watched the car move down the long/unbending/ street. It was her first spring in Indianapolis. She wondered if it wud be beautiful.

He wuz holding her. Crying in her ear. Loud cries, almost louder than the noise already turning in her head. Yeh. He sed between the cries that he had messed up the money. He had . . . he had . . . oh babee. *C'mon Sandy and talk. Talk to me. Help me, babee. Help me to tell you what I got to tell you for both our sakes.* He stretched her out on the green/oversized/couch that sat out from the wall like some displaced trailer waiting to be parked.

I'm hooked, he sed. I'm hooked again on stuff. It's not like befo though when I wuz 17 and just beginning. This time it's different. I mean it has to do now wid me and all my friends who are still on junk. You see I got out of the joint and looked around and saw those brothers who are my friends all still on the stuff and I cried inside. I cried long tears for some beautiful dudes who didn't know how the man had 'em by they balls. Baby I felt so sorry for them and they wuz so turned around that one day over to Tony's crib I got high wid 'em. That's all babee. I know I shouldn't have done that. You and the kids and all. But they wuz dudes I wuz in the joint wid. My brothers who wuz still unaware. I can git clean, babee. I mean, I don't have a long jones. I ain't been on it too long. I can kick now. Tomorrow. You just say it. Give me the word/sign that you understand, forgive me for being one big asshole and I'll start kicking tomorrow. For you babee. I know I been laying some heavy stuff on you. Spending money we ain't even got—I'll git a job too next week—staying out all the time. Hitting you fo telling me the truth 'bout myself. My actions. Babee, it's you I love in spite of my crazy actions. It's you I love. Don't nobody else mean to me what you do. It's just that I been acting crazy but I know I can't keep on

38

keepin' on this way and keep you and the children. Give me a whole lot of slack during this time and I can kick it, babee. I love you. You so good to me. The meanest thing that done ever happened to me. You the best thing that ever happened to me in all of my 38 years and I'll take better care of you. Say something Sandy. Say you understand it all. Say you forgive me. At least that, babee.

He raised her head from the couch and kissed her. It was a short cooling kiss. Not warm. Not long. A binding kiss. She opened her eyes and looked at him, and the bare room that somehow now complemented their lives, and she started to cry again. And as he grabbed her and rocked her, she spoke fo the first time since she had told that wite/collar/man in the bank that the bank was wrong.

The-the-the-the bab-bab-bab-ies. Ar-ar-ar-are th-th-th-they o-o-okay? Oh my god. I'm stuttering. Stuttering, she thot. Just like when I wuz little. Stop talking. Stop talking girl. Write what you have to say. Just like you used to when you wuz little and you got tired of people staring at you while you pushed words out of an unaccommodating mouth. Yeh. That was it, she thot. Stop talking and write what you have to say. Nod yo/head to all of this madness. But rest yo/head and use yo/hands till you git it all straight again.

She pointed to her bag and he handed it to her. She took out a pen and notebook and wrote that she wuz tired, that her head hurt and wuz spinning, and that she wanted to sleep fo awhile. She turned and held his face full of little sores where he had picked fo ingrown hairs the nite befo. She kissed them and let her tongue move over his lips, wetting them. He smiled at her and sed he wud git her a couple sleeping pills. He wud also pick up some dollies fo himself cuz Saturday was kicking time fo him. As he went out the door he turned and sed, *Lady, you some lady. I'm a lucky M.F. to have found you.* She watched him from the window and the sun hit the gold of his dashiki and made it bleed yellow raindrops.

She must have dozed. She knew it wuz late. It was dark out-side. The room was dark also and she wondered if he had come in and gone upstairs where the children were napping. What a long nap the boys were taking. They wud be up all nite tonite if they didn't wake up soon. Maybe she shud wake them up, but she decided against it. Her body wuz still tired and she heard footsteps on the porch.

His voice was light and cracked a little as he explained his delay. He wuz high. She knew it. He sounded like he sounded on the phone when he called her late in the nite from some loud place and complimented her fo understanding his late hours. She hadn't understood them, she just hated to be a complaining bitch. He had no sleeping pills, but he had gotten her something as good. A morphine tablet. She watched his face as he explained that she cud swallow it or pop it into the skin. He sed it worked better if you stuck it in yo/arm. As he took the tablet out of the cellophane paper of his cigarettes, she closed her eyes and fo a moment, she thot she heard someone crying outside the house. She opened her eyes.

His body hung loose as he knelt by the couch. He took from his pocket a manila envelope. It had little spots of blood on it and as he undid the rubber hands, she saw two needles, a black top wid two pieces of dirty, wite cotton balls in it. She knew this wuz what he used to git high wid.

I-I-I-I-I don-don-don-don't wa-wa-want none o-o-o-of that stuff, ma-a-a-a-n. Ain't th-th-th-that do-do-do- dope, too? I-I-I-I-I just just just just wa-wa-wa-nnnt-ted to sleep. I'm o-o-o-kay now. She picked up her notebook and pen and started to write again.

I slept while you wuz gone, man. I drifted on off as I looked for yo to walk up the steps. I don't want that stuff. Give me a cold beer though, if there's any in the house. I'll drink that. But no stuff man, she wrote. I'm yo/woman. You shudn't be giving me any of that stuff. Throw the pill away. We don't need it. You don't need it any mo. You gon kick and we gon move on. Keep on being baddDDD togetha. I'll help you, man, cuz I know you want to kick. Flush it down the toilet! You'll start kicking tomorrow and I'll get a babysit-ter and take us fo a long drive in the country and we'll move on the grass and make it move wid us, cuz we'll be full of living/alive/ thots and we'll stop and make love in the middle of nowhere, and the grass will stop its wintry/brown/chants and become green as our Black bodies sing. Heave. Love each other. Throw that stuff away, man, cuz we got more important/beautiful/things to do.

As he read the note his eyes looked at hers in a half/clear/ way and he got up and walked slowly to the john. She heard the toilet flushing and she heard the refrigerator door open and close. He brought two cold beers and, as she opened hers, she sat up to watch him rock back and forth in the rocking chair. And his eyes became small and sad as he sed, half-jokingly, *Hope I don't regret throwing that stuff in the toilet*, and he leaned back and smiled sadly as he drank his beer. She turned the beer can up to her lips and let the cold evening foam wet her mouth and drown the gathering stutters of her mind.

The sound of cries from the second floor made her move. As she climbed the stairs she waved to him. But his eyes were still closed. He wuz somewhere else, not in this house she thot. He wuz somewhere else, floating among past dreams she had never seen or heard him talk about. As she climbed the stairs, the boys' screams grew louder. Wow. Them boys got some strong lungs, she thot. And smiled.

It wuz 11:30 and she had just put the boys in their cribs. She heard them sucking on their bottles, working hard at nourishing themselves. She knew the youngest twin wud finish his bottle first and cry out fo more milk befo he slept. She laughed out loud. He sho cud grease.

He wuz in the bathroom. She knocked on the door, but he sed for her not to come in. She stood outside the door, not moving, and knocked again. Go and turn on the TV, he sed, I'll be out in a few minutes.

It wuz 30 minutes later when he came out. His walk wuz much faster than befo and his voice wuz high, higher than the fear moving over her body. She ran to him, threw her body against him and held on. She kissed him hard and moved her body 'gainst him til he stopped and paid attention to her movements. They fell to the floor. She felt his weight on her as she moved and kissed him. She wuz feeling good and she cudn't understand why he stopped. In the midst of pulling off her dress he stopped and took out a cigarette and lit it while she undressed to her bra and panties. She felt naked all of a sudden and sat down and drew her legs up against her chest and closed her eyes. She reached for a cigarette and lit it.

He stretched out next to her. She felt very ashamed, as if she had made him do something wrong. She wuz glad that she cudn't talk cuz that way she didn't have to explain. He ran his hand up and down her legs and touched her soft wet places.

It's just, babee, that this stuff kills any desire for THAT! I mean, I want you and all that but I can't quite git it up to perform. He lit another cigarette and sat up. *Babee, you sho know how to pick 'em. I mean, wuz you born under an unlucky star or sumthin'? First, you had a niggah who preferred a rich/wite/woman to you and Blackness. Now you have a junkie who can't even satisfy you when you need satisfying.* And his laugh wuz harsh as he sed again, *You sho know how to pick 'em, lady.* She didn't know what else to do so she smiled a nervous smile that made her feel, remember times when she wuz little and she had stuttered thru a sentence and the listener had acknowledged her accomplishment wid a smile and all she cud do was smile back.

He turned and held her and sed, *Stay up wid me tonite, babee. I got all these memories creeping in on me. Bad ones. They's the things that make kicking hard, you know. You begin remembering all the mean things you've done to yo/family/friends who dig you. I'm remembering now all the heavee things I done laid on you in such a short time. You hardly had a chance to catch yo/breath when I'd think of sum new game to lay on you. Help me, Sandy.*

Listen to my talk. Hold my hand when I git too sad. Laugh at my fears that keep poppin' out on me like some childhood disease. Be my vaccine, babee. I need you. Don't ever leave me, babee, cuz I'll never have a love like you again. I'll never have another woman again if you leave me. He picked up her hands and rubbed them in his palms as he talked, and she listened until he finally slept and morning crept in through the shades and covered them.

He threw away his works when he woke up. He came over to where she wuz feeding the boys and kissed her and walked out to the backyard and threw the manila envelope into the middle can. He came back inside, smiled and took a dollie wid a glass of water, and fell on the couch.

Sandy put the boys in their strollers in the backyard where she cud watch them as she cleaned the kitchen. She saw Snow, their big/wite/dog, come round the corner of the house to sit in front of them. They babbled words to him but he sat still guarding them from the backyard/evils of the world.

She moved fast in the house, had a second cup of coffee, called their babysitter and finished straightening up the house. She put on a short dress which showed her legs, and she felt good about her black/hairy legs. She laughed as she remembered that the young brothers on her block used to call her a big/legged/momma as she walked in her young ways.

They never made the country. Their car refused to start and Winston wuz too sick to push it to the filling station for a jump. So they walked to the park. He pushed her in the swing and she pumped herself higher and higher and higher till he told her to stop. She let the swing come slowly to a stop and she jumped out

44

and hit him on the behind and ran. She heard him gaining on her and she tried to dodge him but they fell laughing and holding each other. She looked at him and her eyes sed, *I wish you cud make love to me man.* As she laughed and pushed him away she thot, *but just you wait til you all right Winston, I'll give you a workout you'll never forget,* and they got up and walked till he felt badly and went home.

He stayed upstairs while she cooked. When she went upstairs to check on him, he was curled up, wrapped tight as a child in his mother's womb. She wiped his head and body full of sweat and kissed him and thought how beautiful he wuz and how proud she wuz of him. She massaged his back and went away. He called fo her as she wuz feeding the children and asked for the wine. He needed somethin' else to relieve this saturday/nite/pain that was creeping up on him. He looked bad, she thot, and raced down the stairs and brought him the sherry. He thanked her as she went out the door and she curtsied, smiled and sed, *Any ol time, man.* She noticed she hadn't stuttered and felt good.

By the time she got back upstairs he was moaning and fuming back and forth on the bed. He had drunk half the wine in the bottle, now he wuz getting up to bring it all up. When she came back up to the room he sed he was cold, so she got another blanket for him. He wuz still cold, so she took off her clothes and got under the covers wid him and rubbed her body against him. She wuz scared. She started to sing a Billie Holiday song. *Yeh. God bless the child that's got his own.* She cried in between the lyrics as she felt his big frame trembling and heaving. *Oh god,* she thot, *am I doing the right thing?* He soon quieted down and got up to go to the toilet. She closed her eyes as she waited fo him. She closed her eyes and felt the warmth of the covers creeping over her. She remembered calling his name as she drifted off to sleep. She remembered how quiet everything finally wuz.

One of the babies woke her up. She went into the room, picked up his bottle and got him more milk. It wuz while she wuz handing him the milk that she heard the silence. She ran to their bedroom and turned on the light. The bed wuz empty. She ran down the stairs and turned on the lights. He was gone. She saw her purse on the couch. Her wallet woz empty. Nothing was left. She opened the door and went out on the porch, and she remembered the lights were on and that she wuz naked. But she stood fo a moment looking out at the flat/Indianapolis/street and she stood and let the late/nite/air touch her body and she turned and went inside.

BEYOND THE FALLOUT

mimi se wewe

Bluebirdbluebirdthrumywindow

denn die einen sind im Dunkeln
(some there are who live in darkness)
und die andern sind im Licht
(while the others live in light)
und man sichet die im Lichte
(we see those who live in daylight)
die im Dunkeln sieht man nicht
(those in darkness out of sight)

—BERTOLT BRECHT

And the Supreme Court said housing and welfare are not fundamental rights.

The right to vote, marry and procreate are the only fundamental rights.

Question: What rights are considered fundamental?

Answer: Only those rights essential to our concept of ordered liberty.

Question: What do you mean? Make it plain, girl. Make it plain.

Answer: In other words, a democratic society without these rights would not be considered civilized. If you don't have 'em, you ain't civilized.

Isn't it lovely to be civilized?

You've seen her. You know you have. She sits on cardboard at Broad and Columbia in front of Zavelle's. Four coats layer her body. Towels are wrapped with a rope around her feet to keep them warm. A plastic bag full of her belongings stands in formation next to her. She's anywhere between 40 and 70 years old. A grey Black woman of North Philadelphia. Sitting sharply. Watching the whirl of people pass by, she sits through winter, spring, summer, fall and law students keeping time to memory.

You've seen her. You know you have. The old woman walking her ulcerated legs down Market street; the old harridan mumbling pieces of a dead dream as she examines garbage can after garbage can.

"Hey there, girlie. Can you spare me a quarter? I ain't eaten in four days. C'mon now, honey. Just one little quarter."

So you give her a quarter and keep on walking to your apartment. So you hand her the money that relieves you of her past present and future. Onward Christian country marching off as to war, with your cross behind you, going as before.

She was turning the corner of the rest room at Pennsylvania Station as I came out of the stall. It was 10:59 p.m., and I was waiting for the 11:59 p.m. to Philadelphia. She entered the bathroom, walking her swollen black feet, dragging her polka-dot feet in blue house slippers.

Her cape surrounded her like a shroud. She grunted herself down underneath one of the hand dryers.

I watched her out of the corner of my eyes as I washed and dried my hands. What did she remind me of? This cracked body full of ghosts. This beached black whale. This multilayered body gathering dust.

Whose mother are you? Whose daughter were you for so many years? What grandchild is standing still in your eyes? What is your name, old black woman of bathrooms and streets?

She opened her dirty sheet of belongings and brought out an old plastic bowl. She looked up and signaled to me.

"Hey you. There. Yeah. You. Miss. Could you put some water in this here bowl for me please? It's kinda hard for me to climb back up once I sits down here for the night."

I took the bowl and filled it with water. There was no hot water, only cold. I handed it to her, and she turned the bowl up to her mouth and drank some of the water. Then she began the slow act of taking off her slippers and socks. The socks numbered six. They were all old and dirty. But her feet. A leper's feet. Cracked. Ulcerated. Peeling with dirt and age.

She baptized one foot and then the other with water. Yes. Wash the "souls" of your feet, my sister. Baptize them in bathroom water. We're all holy here.

You've seen her. You know you have. Sitting in the lower chambers of the garage. Guarding the entering and exiting cars. Old black goddess of our American civilization at its peak.

She sits still as a Siamese. Two shopping bags surround her like constant lovers. She sits on two blankets. A heavy quilt is wrapped around her body.

"Good morning, sister." I scream against the quiet. Her eyes. Closed. Open into narrow slits. Yellow sleep oozes out of her eyes. Then a smile of near-recognition. A smile of gratitude perhaps. Here I am, her smile announces, in the upper sanctum of

51

Manhattan. A black Siamese for these modern monuments. Let those who would worship at my shrine come now or forever hold their peace. Hee. Hee. Hee.

She leans toward me and says, "Glorious morning, ain't it? You has something for yo' ole sister today? For yo' old mother?"

The blue and white morning stretches her wings across the dying city. I lean forward and give her five dollars. The money disappears under her blanket as she smiles a lightning smile. Her eyes open and for the first time I see the brown in her eyes. Brown-eyed woman. She looks me in the eye and says, "Don't never go to sleep on the world, girl. Whiles you sleeping the world scrambles on. Keep yo' eyes open all the time."

Then she closes her eyes and settles back into a sinister still-ness. I stand waiting for more. After all, we have smiled at each other for years. I have placed five dollars regularly into her hand. I wait. She does not move, and finally I walk on down the street. What were you waiting for girl? What more could she possibly say to you that you don't already know? Didn't you already know who and what she was from her voice, from her clothes? Hadn't you seen her for years on the streets and in the doorways of America? Didn't you recognize her?

I walk the long block to my apartment. It will be a long day. I feel exhausted already. Is it the New York air? My legs become uncoordinated. Is it the rhythm of the city that tires me so this morning? I must find a chair, or curb, a doorway to rest on. My legs are going every which way but up.

I find a doorway on Broadway. I lean. Close my eyes to catch my morning breath. Close my mouth to silence the screams moving upward like vomit.

She was once somebody's mama. I ain't playing the dozens. She was once someone's child toddling through the playgrounds of America in tune to bluebirdbluebird thru my window, bluebirdbluebird thru my window.

Where do the bluebirds go when they're all used up?

HAIKU

i see you blackboy
bent toward destruction watching
for death with tight eyes

I HAVE WALKED
A LONG TIME

i have walked a long time
much longer than death that splinters
wid her innuendos.
my life, ah my alien life,
is like an echo of nostalgia
bringen blue screens to bury clouds
rinsen wite stones stretched among the sea.

> *you, man, will you remember me when i die?*
> *will you stare and stain my death and say*
> *i saw her dancen among swallows*
> *far from the world's obscenities?*
> *you, man, will you remember and cry?*

and i have not loved.
always
while the body prowls
the soul catalogues each step;
while the unconscious unbridles feasts
the flesh knots toward the shore.
ah, i have not loved
wid legs stretched like stalks against sheets

wid stomachs drainen the piracy of oceans
wid mouths discarden the gelatin
to shake the sharp self.
i have walked by memory of others
between the blood night
and twilights
i have lived in tunnels
and fed the bloodless fish;
between the yellow rain
and ash,
i have heard the rattle
of my seed,
so time, like some pearl necklace embracen
a superior whore, converges
and the swift spider binds my breast.

you, man, will you remember me when i die?
will you stare and stain my death and say
i saw her applauden suns
far from the grandiose audience?
you, man, will you remember and cry?

KALEIDOSCOPE

tumbling blue and brown
tulips that leap
into frogs
women dancing in metal
blue raindrops sliding
into green diamonds
turtles crawling outward
into stars
electric w's
spreading beyond words
papooses turning
into hearts
and butterflies stretching
into court jesters
who jump
amid red splinters
just like you.

ON PASSING
THRU MORGANTOWN, PA.

i saw you

vincent van

gogh perched

on those pennsylvania

cornfields communing

amid secret black

bird societies. yes.

i'm sure that was

you exploding your

fantastic delirium

while in the

distance

red indian

hills beckoned.

MASKS

"blacks don't have the intellectual capacity to succeed."

—WILLIAM COORS

the river runs toward day
and never stops.
so life receives the lakes
patrolled by one-eyed pimps
who wash their feet in our blue whoredom

the river floods
the days grow short
we wait to change our masks
we wait for warmer days and
fountains without force
we wait for seasons without power.

today
ah today
only the shrill sparrow seeks the sky
our days are edifice.
we look toward temples that give birth to sanctioned flesh.

                              o bring the white mask
                              full of the chalk sky.

entering the temple
on this day of sundays

i hear the word spoken
by the unhurried speaker
who speaks of unveiled eyes.

                              o bring the chalk mask
                                   full of altitudes.

straight in this chair
tall in an unrehearsed role
i rejoice
and the spirit sinks in twilight of
distant smells.

                              o bring the mask
                              full of drying blood.

fee, fie, fo, fum,
i smell the blood
of an englishman

O my people
wear the white masks
for they speak without speaking
and hear words of forgetfulness.

o my people.

ON SEEING
A PACIFIST BURN

this day is not
real. the crowing of
the far-away
carillons ring
out direction
less. even you are
un real roasting
under a man
hattan sky
while passersby flap
their indecent tongues.
even i am un
real but i
am black and
thought to be
without meaning.

TRAVELING ON AN AMTRAK TRAIN COULD HUMANIZE YOU

I saw him enter the train. His walk announced a hipster for all seasons; his clothing said doorways, hunger and brawls. A lifetime of insults.

I immediately put my large brown bag on the seat next to mine, lowered my eyes, turned my head to peer out at the figures rushing to catch the train to NYC. From Newark to NYC in one short easy ride.

He looked at me, nodded, walked to the seat behind me. I heard the seat collapse with his weight, heard the tight intake of breath from the businessman who pulled himself up straight as white lace.

His voice was loud but strangely soft as he said, "Let me see your hands, man. They're smooth as ice. You ain't never worked a hard day in your life, have you man? Where you go to school? Harvard? You make big money, I bet. Don't cha? I have a high school diploma. Are you in hiring? My name's Herbert. What's yours?"

The stillness caressed the red-cushioned car crashing against the chatter of Thursday afternoon commuters, students and shoppers.

He continued. "I ain't drunk or crazy. I just like talking to people, successful people like you. I like to know what you about. What it feels like to have made it. What kind of job you got? You in a big corporation or something, ain't ya?"

The businessman stirred in his seat. He cleared his throat of all tentative sounds and then words darted from his tongue so fast I heard centuries passing through his voice.

"I'm a securities analyst for a firm in New York, and I make enough (nervous laugh) to take care of the family. No, I'm not hiring at all. My name is John Glantz, though. Glad to meet you, ahem, Herbert. Very glad to meet you."

I heard the shaking of hands, their voices momentarily silenced by their hands shaking in tune to color and noise. Questions and answers.

"Told you your hands were soft."

Herbert's short laugh bounced from his lips with ease. "My hands," he continued, "are certified razors. Go on, touch them. Feel them. They won't bite 'less I say sic' em. Go on, feel them, man. They so rough they might cut you in two."

And again the sound of a voice, higher and clearer than before. A voice moving across years like freshly polished silver. A voice circling new terrain.

"Yes. They are quite rough, but strong. A man's hands." The businessman's voice struggled with forced words.

"My ole lady used to feel my hands, you know, and she said keep them hard things offa me, man, they too rough for my body, always laying in ambush for me. She wanted me to have smooth hands like yours. My hands always embarrassed her, calloused by the rhythm of work. She called them alligator hands, she did."

The train charged ahead full tilt, tilting memories. As it leaped and settled inside the tunnel, the light flickered out.

Men and words fused into one slow-moving silence. The silence of darkness. The silence of tension peeling from the windows.

The lights returned.

"Thought you wuz a goner for a moment, didn't ya? Ha! Ha! Naw, man. It ain't that way a-tall. Hey! You ever see Hurricane Carter fight? I used to spar with him some years ago. He was a tough dude, bad in the ring. He could take care of some business. Did you see him fight his last fight?"

"Yes, I did. He was a good fighter. I think I liked Muhammad Ali better, though. My two boys always liked Ali. We used to watch him fight together. They don't watch boxing anymore. They think it's crude and violent. Imagine that. All they play is soccer now."

"You have just the two boys?"

"Yes, just two sons. They're 15 and 14. I don't see them often. They're away at school now."

"I have one son, 14 years old, too. He's a smart young dude. That school ain't teaching him nothing, though. I gotta keep him smart too. Can't have him traveling from Newark to New York everyday for a quick hustle. Anyway, your ass gits worn out ya know from all this traveling everyday. You know what I mean?"

Their laughter traveled down the long carpeted car, bouncing off ears closed by sleep and habit. Their laughter resounded against years of locked doors and minds. Their male laughter came like sea birds tasting new foam.

"Seriously, though. What do you do in New York everyday, Herbert? You have a good head on your shoulders. Why aren't you working?"

"Ain't had a real job in fourteen years, not since I hurt my back 14 years ago. Can't work the way I used to. Harvard. You don't know what it means not to work. I was a man, a father, a husband cocked before the world; now my body sweats in retirement. And they talkin' about taking away my disability payments. How we gonna make it, man? How I'm gonna be a man?"

Silence. Pauses of yellow silence walking barefoot on the train. Voices of people getting ready to disembark, searching the train for traces of themselves.

Here we are, people, I wanted to cry out. Here we are in NYC without the slightest idea of why and who when we ignore the men and women keloiding before us with pain.

Time to reassess before leaving.

I was in my seat watching the train run from Philly to Newark to New York;

There were trains going in opposite directions;

I was alone, but I saw people, hermetically sealed with their own styles of breathing;

I was on a train, and I heard tongues swell and grow;

But I was not alone;

I had come from Graterford, where all the men are immortal;

They never die;

They merely depart or disintegrate down crowded cells;

I had come from Graterford, where they do pilgrimage each day in their cells without incense.

. . . .

I followed the two men up the stairs to Eighth Avenue. They parted. Herbert walked on an Eighth Avenue tide of dancing taxis and flesh. I turned eastward toward the river, toward the U.N. where a geography of men and women gargle with surplus words.

Traveling on an Amtrack train could humanize you.

GRENADES
ARE NOT FREE

a luta continua

BUBBA

How shall I tell you of him. Bubba, young man of Harlem? Bubba. Of filling stations and handball games; of summer bongo playing; of gang bangs; of strict laughter piercing the dark, long summers kept us peeled across stoops looking for air. Bubba. Of gangs who pimped a long walk across Harlem and decided who would pass and who would be stopped at the gateway of life.

Bubba. Black as a panther. Bubba. Whose teeth shone like diamonds while he smiled at us from across his dominion. Who stretched his legs until they snapped in two when his days became shorter and schools sent him out among the world of pushcarts and do rags of Seventh Avenue. Bubba. Who gave his genius up to the temper of the times.

While I marched off to Hunter College and the aroma of Park Avenue; while I marched off to Proust and things unremembered; while I read sociology texts that reminded us few Blacks that we were aberrations of the world; Bubba, and other marched off to days of living in a country that said, "I'm the greatest hustler in the world so don't come downtown trying to hustle me. Hustle your own."

And he did. And they did.

"Hey there, pretty lady. Yeah. You strutting yo' young black ass 'cross 125th street. I be digging on you. See that corner over there baby? Stretch out on that corner so we can live in the style that we ain't never been accustomed to. Want to be accustomed to."

And she did. And they did. Young girls throwing their souls on Harlem corners. Standing dead on dead avenues. Caged black birds in a country without age or memory.

One summer day, I remember Bubba and I banging the ball against the filling station. Handball champs we were. The king and queen of the handball we were. And we talked as we played. He asked me if I ever talked to trees or rivers or things like that, and I who walked with voices for years denied the different tongues populating my mouth. I stood still denying the commonplace things of my private childhood. And his eyes pinned me against the filling station wall and my eyes became small and lost their color.

"I hear voices all the time," he said. "I talk to the few trees we have here in Harlem." And then he smiled a smile that kept moving back to some distant time that I stopped looking at him and turned away. I thought I would get lost inside his sorcery.

"When I was real small," he continued, "I used to think that the moon belonged to me, that it came out only for me, that it followed me everywhere I went. And I used to, when it got dark there in North Carolina, I used to run around to the backyard and wait for the moon to appear. And when she came out I would dance a wild dance that woke up my father. My father used to scream outside at me and say, 'Stop that foolishness boy. You ain't got the sense you wuz born with.'" Bubba laughed a laugh that came from a million cells.

"I ain't never told nobody that before. But you so dreamylike girl, always reading, that I thought you would know what it is to walk with drums beating inside you. But you just a brain with no imagination at all. Catch ya later baby. I'm gon go on downtown to a flick."

I nodded my head as he left. I nodded my head as I hit the ball against the wall. I nodded my head as the voices peeped in and out of my ears and nostrils leaving a trail around my waist. I picked myself up from the fear of anyone knowing who I was and went home; never to talk to Bubba again about seeing behind trees and walking over seas with flowers growing out of my head.

Words. Books. Waltzed me to the tune of Hunter College days. I severed all relationships with my block. Each night I drenched myself with words so I could burst through the curtain of Harlem days and nights. My banner was my tongue as I climbed toward the gourds of knowledge and recited a poem of life.

"Hey. There. Girl. How you be? Hear you goin' to Hunter now. How is it?" It was Bubba. Bubba. Of greasy overalls. Of two children screaming for food. Of a wife pregnant with another. Of the same old neighborhood.

"Oh, Hunter's all right Bubba. If you like that sort of thing."

"But what you studying girl? What you studying to be? A teacher? A lawyer? What?"

"Well, I'm studying a little Sociology. Psychology. History. Chemistry. I'm not quite sure just what it is I intend to be. Do you understand?"

"Yeah, I understand. Catch you later girl." And he walked his tired footsteps to the corner bar and went inside.

And I stood outside. Afraid to cross the street, abandoned to the rhythms of America's tom-toms.

One day, after graduation, I returned to the old neighborhood. I recognized a few faces and sat and talked. I was glad to sit down. I had taught all day long. I answered the questions of my former neighbors. And the tension of the years dissolved in our laughter. Just people. Remembering together. Laughing.

"Does Bubba still live 'round here?" I finally asked. The women pointed to the mini-park. And I called out goodbye and walked past the filling station to the park. There he sat. Nodding out the day. The years.

As long as I have hands that write; as long as I have eyes that see; as long as I can bear your name against silence; I shall never forget our last talk Bubba. That September day when I sat next to you and told you my dreams and my prayers.

The air froze as you raised your hand and spoke. "Hey there girl. How . . ." And I continued to talk. Holding your hand, our silence, remembering for you the laughter you gave us so freely, thanking you for the conversations and protection you gave me.

"Hey there girl," he sniffled. "Wanna play some handball and . . ."

And I waited with him on that bench. Watched the sun go down. Saw the moon come out.

"Bubba," I said. "There she is, your old friend the moon. Coming out just for you."

He finally pulled himself up off the bench. He stood up with the last breath of a dying man.

"How 'bout a few bucks girl? Gotta see a man 'bout something."

I handed him $20. He put it in his pocket, scratched his legs and nodded goodbye.

Bubba. If you hadn't fallen off of that roof in '57, you would have loved the '60s. Bubba you would have loved Malcolm. You would have plucked the light from his eyes and finally seen the world in focus.

Bubba. Your footsteps sing around my waist each day. I will not let the country settle into the sleep of the innocent.

A POEM FOR PAUL

your face like
summer lightning
gets caught in my voice
and i draw you up from
deep rivers
taste your face of a
thousand names
see you smile
a new season
hear your voice
a wild sea pausing in the wind.

FROM A BLACK FEMINIST CONFERENCE

Reflections on Margaret Walker: Poet

chicago/october 1977/saturday afternoon/margaret walker walks her red clay mississippi walk into a room of feminists. a strong gust of a woman. raining warm honeysuckle kisses and smiles. and i fold myself into her and hear a primordial black song sailing down the guinea coast.

her face. ordained with lines. confesses poems. halleluyas. choruses. she turns leans her crane-like neck on the edge of the world, emphasizing us. in this hotel/village/room. heavy with women. our names become known to us.

there is an echo about her. of black people rhyming. of a woman celebrating herself and a people. words ripen on her mouth like pomegranates. this pecan/color/woman. short limbed with lightning. and i swallow her whole as she pulls herself up from youth, shaking off those early chicago years where she and wright and others turned a chicago desert into a wellspring of words.

eyes. brilliant/southern eyes torpedoing the room with sun. eyes/ dressed like a woman. seeing thru riddles. offering asylum from ghosts.

she stands over centuries as she talks. hands on waist. a feminine memory washed up from another shore. she opens her coat. a light colored blouse dances against dark breasts. her words carved from ancestral widows rain children and the room contracts with color.

her voice turns the afternoon brown. this black woman poet. removing false veils, baptizes us with syllables. woman words. entering and leaving at will:

> Let a new earth rise. Let another world be born. Let a bloody peace be written in the sky. Let a second generation full of courage issue forth; let a people loving freedom come to growth. Let a beauty full of healing and a strength of final clenching be the pulsing in our spirits and our blood. Let the martial songs be written, let the dirges disappear. Let a race of men now rise and take control.*

walking back to my room, i listen to the afternoon. play it again and again. scatter myself over evening walls and passageways wet with her footprints. in my room i collect papers. breasts. and listen to our mothers hummmmming

---

*"For My People" by Margaret Walker

HAIKU

(written from Peking)

let me wear the day
well so when it reaches you
you will enjoy it

A LETTER TO
EZEKIEL MPHAHLELE

dear zeke,

i've just left your house where you and rebecca served a dinner of peace to me and my sons. the ride home is not as long as the way i came, two centuries of hunger brought me along many detours before i recognized your house. it is raining and as i watch the raindrops spin like colored beads on the windshield, i hear your voice calling out to your ancestors to prepare a place for you, for you were returning home leaving the skeleton rites of twenty years behind.

you and rebecca have been walking a long time. your feet have crossed the african continent to this western one where you moved amid leaden eyes and laughter that froze you in snow/ capped memories. your journey began in 1957, when the ruling class could not understand your yawns of freedom, the motion of a million eyes to see for themselves what life was/is and could be, and you cut across the burial grounds of south africa where many of your comrades slept and you cut across those black africans smiling their long smiles from diplomatic teeth. now you are returning home. now your mother's womb cries out to you. now your history demands your heartbeat. and you turn your body toward the whirlwind of change, toward young black voices calling for a dignity speeding beyond control, on the right side of the road. but this nite full of whispering summer trees, this nite nodding with south african faces, heard you say, sonia. i must be buried in my country in my own homeland, my bones must replenish the black earth from whence they came, our bones must fertilize the ground on which we walk or we shall never walk as men and women in the 21st century.

i talked to my sons as the car chased the longlegged rain running before us. i told them that men and women are measured by their acts not by their swaggering speech or walk, or the money they have stashed between their legs. i talked to my sons about bravery outside of bruce lee grunts and jabs, outside of star wars' knights fertilizing america's green youth into continued fantasies while reality explodes in neutron boldness. i said you have just sat and eaten amid bravery. relish the taste. stir it around and around in your mouth until the quick sweetness of it becomes bitter, then swallow it slowly, letting this new astringent taste burn the throat. bravery is no easy taste to swallow. i said this man and woman we have just left this nite have decided to walk like panthers in their country, to breathe again their own breath suspended by twenty years of exile, to settle in the maternal space of their birth where there are men who "shake hands without hearts" waiting for them. they are a fixed portrait of courage.

it is 2 a.m., my children stretch themselves in dreams, kicking away the room's shadows. i stare at the nite piling in little heaps near my bed. zeke. maybe you are a madman. i a madwoman to want to walk across the sea, to saddle time while singing a future note. we follow the new day's breath, we answer old bruises waiting to descend upon our heads, we answer screams creeping out of holes and shells buried by memories waiting to be cleansed. you invoking the ghosts lurking inside this child/woman. you breaking my curtain of silence. i love the tom-tom days you are marching, your feet rooted in the sea. save a space for me and mine zeke and rebecca. this lost woman, who walks her own shadow for peace.

REFLECTIONS AFTER THE JUNE 12TH MARCH FOR DISARMAMENT

I have come to you tonite out of the depths
    of slavery
    from white hands peeling black skins over
    america;
I have come out to you from reconstruction eyes
    that closed on black humanity
    that reduced black hope to the dark
    huts of america;
I have come to you from the lynching years,
    the exploitation of black men and women by
    a country that allowed the swinging of
    strange fruits from southern trees;
I have come to you tonite thru the
    delaney years, the du bois years,
    the b.t. washington years, the robeson
    years, the garvey years, the
    depression years, the you can't eat
    or sit or live just die here years,
    the civil rights years, the black power
    years, the black nationalist years, the
    affirmative action years, the liberal
    years, the neoconservative years;

I have come to say that those years
        were not in vain, the ghosts of our
        ancestors searching this american dust for
        rest were not in vain, black women
        walking their lives in clots were not
        in vain, the years walked
        sideways in a forsaken land were not
        in vain;
I have come to you tonite as an equal,
        as a comrade, as a black woman
        walking down a corridor of tears,
        looking neither to the left or the right,
        pulling my history with bruised
        heels,
        beckoning to the illusion of america
        daring you to look me in the eyes to
        see these faces, the exploitation of a
        people because of skin pigmentation;
I have come to you tonite because no people
        have been asked to be modern day people
        with the history of slavery, and still
        we walk, and still we talk, and
        still we plan, and still we hope and
        still we sing;
I have come to you tonite because there are
        inhumanitarians in the world. they are not
        new. they are old. they go back into history.
        they were called explorers, soldiers, mercenaries,

imperialists, missionaries, adventurers,
but they looked at the world for what
it would give up to them and they violated
the land and the people, they looked
at the land and sectioned it up for
private ownership, they looked at the
people and decided how to manipulate
them thru fear and ignorance, they looked
at the gold and began to hoard and
worship it;

I have come to you because it is time
for us all to purge capitalism from
our dreams, to purge materialism
from our eyes, from the planet earth
to deliver the earth again into the hands
of the humanitarians;

I have come to you tonite not just for the stoppage
of nuclear proliferation, nuclear
plants, nuclear bombs, nuclear
waste, but to stop the proliferation
of nuclear minds, of nuclear generals
of nuclear presidents, of nuclear scientists,
who spread human and nuclear waste
over the world;

I come to you because the world needs to be
saved for the future generations who must
return the earth to peace, who will not
be startled by a man's/woman's skin color;

come to you because the world needs sanity
now, needs men and women who will
not work to produce nuclear weapons,
who will give up their need for excess
wealth and learn how to share the
world's resources, who will never
again as scientists invent again just
for the sake of inventing;
come to you because we need to turn our
eyes to the beauty of this planet, to the
bright green laughter of trees, to the beautiful
human animals waiting to smile their unprostituted smiles;
I have come to you to talk about our inexperience
at living as human beings, thru death marches and camps
thru middle passages and slavery
and thundering countries raining hungry faces;
I am here to move against leaving
our shadows implanted on the
earth while our bodies disintegrate in
nuclear lightning;
I am here between the voices of our ancestors
and the noise of the planet,
between the surprise of death and life;
I am here because I shall not give the
earth up to nondreamers and earth molesters;
I am here to say to you:
my body is full of veins
like the bombs waiting to burst

with blood.
we must learn to suckle life not
bombs and rhetoric
rising up in redwhiteandblue patriotism;
I am here. and my breath/our breaths
must thunder across this land
arousing new breaths. new life.
new people, who will live in peace
and honor.

A LETTER TO
DR. MARTIN LUTHER KING

Dear Martin,

Great God, what a morning, Martin!

The sun is rolling in from faraway places. I watch it reaching out, circling these bare trees like some reverent lover, I have been standing still listening to the morning, and I hear your voice crouched near hills, rising from the mountain tops, breaking the circle of dawn.

You would have been 54 today.

As I point my face toward a new decade, Martin, I want you to know that the country still crowds the spirit. I want you to know that we still hear your footsteps setting out on a road cemented with black bones. I want you to know that the stuttering of guns could not stop your light from crashing against cathedrals chanting piety while hustling the world.

Great God, what a country, Martin!

The decade after your death docked like a spaceship on a new planet. Voyagers all we were. We were the aliens walking up the '70s, a holocaust people on the move looking out from dark eyes. A thirsty generation, circling the peaks of our country for more than a Pepsi taste. We were youngbloods, spinning hip syllables while saluting death in a country neutral with pain.

And our children saw the mirage of plenty spilling from capitalistic sands.

And they ran toward the desert.

And the gods of sand made them immune to words that strengthen the breast.

And they became scavengers walking on the earth.

And you can see them playing. Hide-and-go-seek robbers. Native sons. Running on their knees. Reinventing slavery on asphalt. Peeling their umbilical cords for a gold chain.

And you can see them on Times Square, in N.Y.C., Martin, selling their 11-, 12-year-old, 13-, 14-year-old bodies to suburban forefathers.

And you can see them on Market Street in Philadelphia bobbing up bellywise, young fishes for old sharks,

And no cocks are crowing on those mean streets.

Great God, what a morning it'll be someday, Martin!

That decade fell like a stone on our eyes. Our movements. Rhythms. Loves. Books. Delivered us from the night, drove out the fears keeping some of us hoarse. New births knocking at the womb kept us walking.

We crossed the cities while a backlash of judges tried to turn us into moles with blackrobed words of reverse racism. But we knew. And our knowing was like a sister's embrace. We crossed the land where famine was fed in public. Where black stomachs exploded on the world's dais while men embalmed their eyes and tongues in gold. But we knew. And our knowing squatted from memory.

Sitting on our past, we watch the new decade dawning. These are strange days, Martin, when the color of freedom becomes disco fever; when soap operas populate our Zulu braids; as the world turns to the conservative right and general hospitals are closing in Black neighborhoods and the young and the restless are drugged by early morning reefer butts. And houses tremble.

These are dangerous days, Martin, when cowboy-riding presidents corral Blacks (and others) in a common crown of thorns; when nuclear-toting generals recite an alphabet of blood; when multinational corporations assassinate ancient cultures while inaugurating new civilizations. Come out come out, wherever you are. Black country. Waiting to be born . . .

But, Martin, on this, your 54th birthday—with all the reversals—we have learned that black is the beginning of everything.

it was black in the universe before the sun;

it was black in the mind before we opened our eyes;

it was black in the womb of our mother;

black is the beginning,

and if we are the beginning we will be forever.

Martin. I have learned too that fear is not a Black man or woman. Fear cannot disturb the length of those who struggle against material gains for self-aggrandizement. Fear cannot disturb the good of people who have moved to a meeting place where the pulse pounds out freedom and justice for the universe.

Now is the changing of the tides, Martin. You forecast it where leaves dance on the wings of man. Martin. Listen. On this your 54th year, listen and you will hear the earth delivering up curfews

to the missionaries and assassins. Listen. And you will hear the
tribal songs:

Ayeeee	*Ayooooo*	*Ayeee*
Ayeeee	*Ayooooo*	*Ayeee*
Malcolm . . .		*Ke wa rona**
Robeson . . .		*Ke wa rona*
Lumumba . . .		*Ke wa rona*
Fannie Lou . . .		*Ke wa rona*
Garvey . . .		*Ke wa rona*
Johnbrown . . .		*Ke wa rona*
Tubman . . .		*Ke wa rona*
Mandela . . .		*Ke wa rona*

(free Mandela,
free Mandela)

Ássata . . .		*Ke wa rona*

As we go with you to the sun,
as we walk in the dawn, turn our eyes

Eastward and let the prophecy come true
and let the prophecy come true.
Great God, Martin, what a morning it will be!

---

*Ke wa rona: He is ours

MIAS

(missing in action and other atlantas)

this morning i heard the cuckoo bird calling
and i saw children wandering like quicksand
over the exquisite city
scooping up summer leaves in enema bags
self-sustaining warriors spitting
long metal seeds on porcelain bricks.

atlanta:

> city of cathedrals and colleges
> rustling spirituals in the morning air
> while black skulls splinter the nite
> and emmett till bones drop in choruses.

littleman. where you running to?
yes. you. youngblood.
touching and touched at random
running towards places where legions ride.

> yo man. you want some action.
> im yo/main man.
> buy me. i can give it to you
> wholesale.

heyladycarryyobagsfoyou?
50¢costyouonly50¢.yo.man.
washyocar.idoagoodjob.
heymanwhyyousocold?
yoman.youneedyobasement
cleaned?meandmypartner
doyoupdecent. yoman.

johannesburg:

       squatting like a manicured mannequin
       while gathering ghosts clockwise
       and policing men, using up their tongues
       Pronounce death syllables
       in the nite,

        august 18:
       30 yr. old african arrested
       on the highway. taken to
       port elizabeth. examined.
       found to be in good health.
       placed in a private cell
       for questioning.

        sept. 7:
       varicose cells. full of
       assassins, beating their
       red arms against the walls.
       and biko, trying to ration

his blood spills permanent
blood in a port elizabeth cell.
and biko's body sings heavy
with cracks.

    sept. 13:
hear ye. hear ye. hear ye.
i regret to announce that stephen
biko is dead. he has refused
food since sept. 5th. we did
all we could for the man.

he has hanged himself while sleeping
we did all we could for him.
he fell while answering our questions
we did all we could for the man.
he washed his face and hung him
self out to dry
we did all we could for him.
he drowned while drinking his supper
we did all we could for the man.
he fell
        hangedhimself   starved
drowned himself
we did all we could for him.
it's hard to keep someone alive
who won't even cooperate.
hear ye.

can i borrow yo/eyes south africa?
can i redistribute yo/legs america?
multiplying multinationally over the world.

> yebo madoda*
> yebo bafazi
> i say
> yebo madoda
> yebo bafazi

el salvador:
> country of vowelled ghosts.
> country of red bones
> a pulse beat gone mad
> with death.
> redwhiteandblue guns splintering the nite with glass
> redwhiteandblue death squads running on borrowed
> knees cascading dreams.

> quiero ser libre
> pues libre naci
> > i say
> quiero ser libre
> pues libre naci

they came to the village that nite. all day the
birds had pedaled clockwise drowning their

---

yebo madoda: come on men and women

feet in clouds. the old men and women
talked of foreboding, that it was a bad sign.
and they crossed themselves in two as
their eyes concluded design.
they came that nite to the village.
calling peace. liberty. freedom.
their tongues lassoing us with
circus patriotism
their elbows wrapped in blood paper
they came penises drawn
their white togas covering their
stained glass legs
their thick hands tattooing decay
on los campaneros till their
young legs rolled out from under them
to greet death
they came leaving a tattoo of hunger
over the land.

       quiero ser libre

       pues libre naci

so i plant myself in the middle
of my biography
of dying drinking working dancing people
their tongues swollen with slavery
waiting and i say
yebo madoda
yebo bafazi
cmon men and women

peel your guerrilla veins toward
this chorus line of beasts who will sell
the morning air passing thru your bones
cmon. men. and. women.
plant yourself in the middle of your
blood with no transfusions for
reagan or botha or bush or
d'aubuisson.

plant yourself in the eyes of
the children who have died carving out their
own childhood.
plant yourself in the dreams of the people
scattered by morning bullets.
let there be everywhere our talk.
let there be everywhere our eyes.
let there be everywhere our thoughts.
let there be everywhere our love.
let there be everywhere our actions.
breathing hope and victory
into their unspoken questions
summoning the dead to life again
to the hereafter of freedom.

cmon. men. women,
i want to be free.

ABOUT
THE AUTHOR

Poet, playwright, educator, and activist Sonia Sanchez is the author of sixteen books, including *Homecoming, We a BaddDDD People, Love Poems, Homegirls & Handgrenades, I've Been a Woman, Under a Soprano Sky, Wounded in the House of a Friend, Does Your House Have Lions?, Like the Singing Coming Off the Drums, Shake Loose My Skin, Morning Haiku,* and *Collected Poems.* She has edited several anthologies and contributed to dozens more.

Among hundreds of honors she has received over her long and rich career are the National Endowment for the Arts fellowship, the Lucretia Mott Award, the Peace and Freedom Award, a Ford Freedom Scholar Award from the Charles H. Wright Museum of African American History, and a Pew Fellowship in the Arts. She is also the recipient of the Langston Hughes Poetry Award, the Robert Frost Medal, the Wallace Stevens Award, the Dorothy and Lillian Gish Prize, the Jackson Poetry Prize, the Edward MacDowell Medal, and the Anisfield-Wolf Lifetime Achievement Award.

Homegirls & Handgrenades won the 1985 American Book Award, and *Does Your House Have Lions?* was a finalist for the National Book Critics Circle Award.

Sonia Sanchez has taught and lectured at over 500 universities and colleges in the United States and has traveled extensively, reading her poetry in Africa, Australia, Cuba, England, the Caribbean, Norway, Canada, and the People's Republic of China. She was the first Presidential Fellow at Temple University in Philadelphia, where she held the Laura Carnell Chair in English until her retirement in 1999.